# HISTORIC SYNAGOGUES

## *of* PHILADELPHIA *&* THE DELAWARE VALLEY

# HISTORIC SYNAGOGUES

## *of* PHILADELPHIA *&* THE DELAWARE VALLEY

JULIAN PREISLER

Charleston London
THE History PRESS

Published by The History Press
Charleston, SC 29403
www.historypress.net



First published 2009

Manufactured in the United States

ISBN 978.1.59629.572.8

Library of Congress Cataloging-in-Publication Data

Preisler, Julian H.
Historic synagogues of Philadelphia and the Delaware Valley / Julian Preisler.
p. cm.
ISBN 978-1-59629-572-8
1. Synagogues--Pennsylvania--Philadelphia Region--Pictorial works. 2. Synagogue architecture--Pennsylvania--Philadelphia Region--Pictorial works. 3. Synagogues--Delaware River Valley (N.Y.-Del. and N.J.)--Pictorial works. 4. Synagogue architecture--Delaware River Valley (N.Y.-Del. and N.J.)--Pictorial works. 5. Judaism--Pennsylvania--Philadelphia Region--History. 6. Judaism--Delaware River Valley (N.Y.-Del. and N.J.)--History. I. Title.
NA4690.P74 2009
296.6'50974811--dc22
2008043207

*Notice*: The information in this book is true and complete to the best of our knowledge. It is offered without guarantee on the part of the author or The History Press. The author and The History Press disclaim all liability in connection with the use of this book.

# CONTENTS

# Acknowledgements

I would like to thank the following institutions and persons for their interest in my project and their willingness to assist by providing photographs, historical data, research leads, etc.: Sarah Sherman, archivist, Philadelphia Jewish Archives; the Jacob Rader Marcus Center of the American Jewish Archives in Cincinnati, Ohio; Gail Pietrzyk, archivist, Jewish Historical Society of Delaware in Wilmington, Delaware; Steven Friedrichs, executive director, Temple Sinai, Dresher, Pennsylvania; Esther Gershman, archives committee chair, Reform Congregation Keneseth Israel, Elkins Park, Pennsylvania; Gavi Miller, executive director, Congregation Adath Jeshurun, Elkins Park, Pennsylvania; John Harris and Sandra Choukroun, Beth Am Israel Congregation, Penn Valley, Pennsylvania; Deborah Sting, PhillyHistory.org and the City of Philadelphia Department of Records; Karen Lewin, education and program director, Congregation Beth El, Yardley, Pennsylvania; Arthur Rosenthol; Walter Spector; Todd Halpern; Julie Miller; Harry Boonin; Steve Shechter; Debbi Albert; Patrica Helfand; and Stephanie and Jim Comfort. I also wish to give special thanks to Richard W. Clark for his unwavering emotional support, editing skills and technical assistance. Thanks are also given to Jonathan Simcosky at The History Press. His patience with my many questions as I went through the process of putting this book together was most appreciated.

# INTRODUCTION

As a researcher, genealogist and archivist, I have always been fascinated by synagogue architecture and the documentation of our Jewish-built environment here in the United States. As far back as I can remember, I have had a keen interest in American synagogues and the variety of architectural styles and designs they reflect. For the past twenty or so years, I have photographed synagogues as a hobby. I have been fortunate to have lived in a variety of cities and states, and I have also had the opportunity to travel to many small towns and cities, especially in the Eastern United States. In 2006, I began to assemble my photographs for a CD-ROM book. The original intent was to share my vast collection of photographs with those interested in synagogue architecture and American Jewish history. What started out as a rather small project grew into an immense collection of synagogue photographs comprising all fifty states and Washington, D.C. The result became volume one of *American Synagogues: A Photographic Journey*.

During this work, I was contacted by The History Press to see if I would be interested in doing a print book of some of my photographs. We chose Philadelphia and the Delaware Valley because of the area's long Jewish community history and variety of synagogue structures. In this book, you will find a unique collection of both current and former synagogues from urban areas and the various suburbs. I had originally hoped to include photographs of as many synagogue buildings as possible, but because of space and time limitations, I had to limit the number featured. Despite this fact, this is probably one of the largest such collections in a book to date. It represents a varied look at all types of synagogues in the area.

This book is not an exhaustive photographic or historical catalogue, but rather a relaxed, informal look at the various styles, sizes and types of synagogues that can be found in Philadelphia and the Delaware Valley. The book covers the city and county of Philadelphia; Bucks, Chester, Delaware and Montgomery Counties in Pennsylvania; Southern New Jersey, including the city of Camden, Cherry Hill Township and Burlington, Camden, Cumberland and Salem Counties; and Wilmington and Newark in New Castle County in Northern Delaware. The focus of this book is the photographs and the buildings they represent, both past and present. Basic historical information on each congregation and building is included to assist the reader in knowing more about a particular building. In many cases, if known, the name of the architect is also included. The historical information on the Jewish communities presented in the following pages is designed to give the reader a brief background and is not meant to present an exhaustive history. There are many excellent local Jewish history books and articles available for those who wish to delve deeper into the Jewish history of the region.

The historical information found in this book comes from my vast collection of synagogue books, Jewish community history books and local history books. Local history, Jewish community and synagogue websites were also helpful to me as I assembled the dates and information about the various buildings and congregations. Many synagogues also took the time to provide information when I requested it. I had hoped for greater participation on the part of local synagogues, but I was grateful for the replies that I received. Particularly helpful with data for the smaller, older Philadelphia congregations was a synagogue history guide created from the research of Allen Meyers, Bunny Kolinsky, Aaron Roetenberg and others. It serves as a sort of genealogical guide to the history of Philadelphia-area synagogues. The resource was created through research at the Philadelphia Jewish Archives Center and is made available through the Jewish Genealogical Society of Greater Philadelphia. There are many varied sources of information available regarding local synagogue history, and the data is often contradictory, but every effort was made to provide as accurate a description as possible.

# Local Jewish Community History

## A Short Introduction

### Philadelphia and Suburbs

Philadelphia boasts one of the largest Jewish communities found in the United States today. Its history is varied and storied, and it has the distinction of being one of the six original Jewish communities that were established in the American colonies. A number of Jewish traders were operating in southeastern Pennsylvania as early as 1703, and there were several Jewish families residing and doing business in the city of Philadelphia by the 1730s. These early Jewish settlers were of Sephardic, and also German, origin. Prominent early Jewish family names included Franks, Gratz, Levy, Salomon and Simon.

The Jewish community's official origins date to 1740, when one of the earliest documented Jewish residents, Nathan Levy, applied to Thomas Penn for a plot to bury his child according to Jewish religious customs. The grant was approved on September 25, 1740, and the plot on Spruce Street between Eighth and Ninth Streets became the first Jewish communal cemetery in Philadelphia—the beginning of organized Jewish life in the colonial city. The first Jewish congregation in Pennsylvania, Congregation Mikveh Israel, traces its beginnings to the establishment of the cemetery in 1740. The new congregation held worship services according to the Sephardic ritual, though by the end of the 1700s the Jewish community was largely Ashkenazic in ethnicity. Mikveh Israel dedicated its first synagogue in 1782 on Cherry Street and Sterling Alley. As more Jews of German origin settled in Philadelphia, desire grew for a congregation that used the Ashkenazic worship ritual. In 1795, Jews from Germany, Holland and Poland organized Congregation Rodeph Shalom, the first Ashkenazic congregation established in the Western Hemisphere. Philadelphia became one of the first cities in the United States to boast two distinct Jewish congregations.

As in other U.S. cities in the early and mid-nineteenth century, Jewish immigration from Germany, Bohemia and Silesia increased, and Jewish communities grew in size. More synagogues and Jewish communal organizations were formed to serve the needs of the growing Jewish population. These German and Bohemian Jews established both Reform and Orthodox synagogues, though many of the Orthodox German synagogues later became Reform. Orthodox Jews from Eastern Europe came in great numbers in the late nineteenth and early twentieth centuries, further increasing the size of most U.S. Jewish communities and establishing synagogues using Eastern European worship rituals.

Philadelphia was no exception. As the population grew and prospered, new congregations were formed. Jews began settling in North, South and West Philadelphia. In the late nineteenth and early twentieth centuries, many of the older and more affluent Jewish congregations built imposing synagogue structures in various areas of North Philadelphia. During the first half of the twentieth century, thriving Jewish communities were located in a variety of areas of Philadelphia. Notable among them were Jewish enclaves in portions of North, Northeast, West and South Philadelphia; Strawberry Mansion; East and West Oak Lane; Logan; Overbrook Park; and Wynnfield. During this time period there were also small, distinct Jewish communities that developed in Chester in Delaware County; Coatesville and West Chester in Chester County; Norristown in Montgomery County; and Bristol and Warrington in Bucks County.

Beginning in the 1950s, as new housing in the suburbs was being developed on a large scale, there was a desire among many in the Jewish community for the new housing and space found in the growing suburbs surrounding the city of Philadelphia. New suburban housing was also being developed within the city limits in Far Northeast Philadelphia. Many congregations relocated to these communities in order to follow their membership. Other congregations merged or closed, and by the 1970s most of the older historic Jewish communities in the city no longer had Jewish populations. Today, large, well-established Jewish communities are found in Center City and Far Northeast, Philadelphia, and in the northern and western suburbs. Some of the largest Jewish communities are found in Montgomery County in Elkins Park and surrounding areas, and also in the Main Line communities of

Wynnewood and Bala Cynwyd. Other expanding Jewish communities can be found in Bucks, Chester and Delaware Counties.

## Camden, Cherry Hill and Southern New Jersey

Jews have lived in New Jersey since the eighteenth century, though a permanent, organized Jewish community did not exist until the arrival of German, Hungarian and Bohemian Jews in the 1840s. The first and oldest Jewish community in the state was established in 1847 in Patterson. Organized as the Congregation B'nai Jeshurun of the Town of Patterson, it was originally Orthodox but later became Reform. B'nai Jeshurun has been located in suburban Franklin Lakes since 1987. While much of the early Jewish settlement and growth was concentrated in the cities and towns west of Newark City, there were also Jewish settlements in the central and southern portions of the state.

The city of Camden, across the Delaware River from Philadelphia, has a long Jewish history. Jews settled there beginning in the 1880s, and at one time there were five Jewish congregations in the city. Congregation Sons of Israel was the earliest congregation to be formed. It was founded in 1894 and was followed by the Shomra Synagogue–Liberty Street Shul, Ahev Zedak Congregation, Congregation Beth El and Congregation Beth Israel. Jews in Camden were active in business, law, real estate and politics, and the Jewish community was a vital part of the city for many years. The Jewish community saw its numbers decline after World War II with the movement to the suburbs and the desire for larger housing and more open space. Further declines occurred after the 1971 riots in Camden.

Today, there are no Jewish congregations in the city, and only three former synagogue buildings remain: Ahev Zedak at 502 Broadway; Beth Israel at Grand Avenue and Benson Street; and the former Sons of Israel Synagogue at Kaighn Avenue and Park Boulevard. The former Talmud Torah, built in 1924, remains at 621 Kaighn Avenue and has been used as a Masonic Center and also a church.

Much of the Jewish movement from Camden was to the suburban area of Cherry Hill Township, first in the western portion and now the eastern portion of that neighborhood. Temple Emanuel and Beth Shalom are located in eastern Cherry Hill, and Congregation Beth El, which is in the eastern portion of the township, is slated to relocate to its newly built synagogue in nearby Voorhees. There were other towns in Camden County and nearby counties that once had synagogues, including Haddon Heights (original location of Beth Sholom), Merchantville, Penns Grove and Willingboro (Levittown). Today, there are Jewish congregations in Cherry Hill, Marlton, Mount Holly, Mount Laurel, Turnersville, Woodbury and elsewhere.

The very southern portion of New Jersey had a unique place in the state's Jewish history because of the many Jewish farming and agricultural communities established there in the late nineteenth and early twentieth centuries. Synagogues were established in towns such as Alliance, Bridgeton, Brotmanville, Carmel, Millville, Rosenhayn, Vineland and Woodbine. A large number of the small synagogues have closed in the last twenty or so years due to severe declines in the Jewish population in these small towns. Some are used as museums or for yearly worship services; others are now used as churches. Vineland is the largest city in Southern New Jersey and still has several operating synagogues. Because of the unique Jewish history that exists in this region, many scholars and researchers are now recording that history. The remaining synagogues and Jewish cemeteries are being photographed, studied and documented, and there are efforts to preserve a number of the structures that are still standing. Many of the synagogues are unique in either their size or style, and interest in them is growing steadily because of threats of demolition or decay due to disuse.

## Wilmington, Newark and Dover, Delaware

Of the thirteen original American colonies, Delaware was the second, after New York, to permit Jews to be admitted legally into the territory. The first Jews believed to have come to Delaware were Isaac Cardoso and Isaac Israel, two traders with the Dutch West India Company in Holland. They arrived in December 1655 and were involved in a variety of business ventures. Few other Jews lived or worked in Delaware during the eighteenth and early nineteenth centuries. Most discontinued actively practicing Judaism or converted to Christianity. Because of the small numbers, no Jewish organizations or groups were formed during this period. The names of some of these early Jews include Jacob Fiana, Daniel Nunez Jr., Abraham Judah and Jacob and Daniel Solis.

It was not until the mid-1850s that more Jews began moving to Delaware, establishing businesses and residences in Wilmington. Most came from

Baltimore and Philadelphia to set up businesses on lower Market Street in central Wilmington. The number of members of the Jewish community was large enough by 1879 that the first Jewish organization in the state was formed—the Moses Montefiore Mutual Benefit Society, an aid society to assist needy members of the Jewish community. This marked the official beginning of the Delaware Jewish community.

The first synagogue services in Delaware were held on the High Holy Days of 1873. The first Jewish congregation, Ohabe Shalom, was established by members of the Montefiore Society in 1880, and a worship space was dedicated in the Morrow Building at 211 North Market Street. The congregation lasted only a few years. In 1885, the first enduring Jewish congregation, the Orthodox Adas Kodesch Congregation, was established. The first permanent synagogue building in the state was dedicated in the summer of 1898, when the congregation acquired the former Zion Lutheran Church at Sixth and French Streets in Wilmington. A historical plaque marks the spot today. The first purpose-built synagogue in Delaware was constructed for the Adas Kodesch Congregation in 1908, when the former building on the site was torn down. The 1908 building no longer stands, however.

Most Jews in Delaware lived in Wilmington proper until the middle of the twentieth century, when people began moving to the suburban areas outside the city limits. There are three Jewish congregations in Wilmington today, and all are located within the city. The buildings have been enlarged and renovated in recent years to meet the needs of the growing congregations. None of the earlier synagogue buildings from the original Jewish settlement remain today. There is also a Jewish congregation in nearby Newark, Delaware, home to the University of Delaware. It was established in the 1950s and is currently the only Reconstructionist Jewish congregation in Delaware.

There has been Jewish settlement in Dover and Kent Counties, Delaware, since the late nineteenth century. Most of these settlers were Jewish farmers or small business owners. It was not until 1947 that an actual Jewish congregation, Beth Sholom, was officially formed in the state capital of Dover. Its current building was constructed in 1963. Beth Sholom of Dover remains a smaller, but vital congregation. In recent years, the Jewish population has been increasing in the resort area of Sussex County. Many Jews from the Baltimore and Washington, D.C. areas have moved there for retirement or have vacation homes there. As a result, a Jewish congregation—the Seaside Jewish Congregation—was formed in the mid-1990s.

Delaware may be one of the smallest states in the nation, but it has a growing and highly organized Jewish community with a rich history and an extensive array of institutions and organizations.

# Local Synagogue Architecture and Style

## Synagogue Architecture in Greater Philadelphia

Philadelphia not only boasts a Jewish community with a long and varied history, but it is also home to many beautiful synagogues, some of which were designed by prominent Jewish, and non-Jewish, architects. Synagogue architecture in Philadelphia, past and present, reflects not only the style trends of the time, but also the needs and budget of each individual congregation. There are no prescribed design requirements for a synagogue's exterior, and Philadelphia-area synagogues were built in a variety of styles and sizes ranging from modest to opulent, plain to exotic. The synagogue structures that exist today in Philadelphia, both current and former, reflect the style trends of the time periods in which they were built. Many of the large and luxurious former synagogue buildings in Philadelphia remain standing today as a testament to the affluence of their congregations.

Two of the very small number of United States synagogues built in the nineteenth-century Egyptian Revival style were built in Philadelphia for Mikveh Israel in 1824 and Beth Israel in 1849. Unfortunately, these buildings no longer survive. The only synagogue designed by world-famous architect Frank Lloyd Wright is Congregation Beth Sholom, located in Elkins Park. Other well-known architects who designed Philadelphia-area synagogues include Arnold Brunner, the Frank Memorial Synagogue in Philadelphia in 1901; Percival Goodman, the current Ohev Shalom synagogue in Wallingford in 1965; Louis I. Kahn, the stark modernist synagogue for

Ahavath Israel of Oak Lane in Philadelphia in 1937; Norman N. Rice, the former Kesher Israel synagogue in West Chester in 1924 and the current Temple Beth Hillel–Beth El in Wynnewood in 1967; noted Philadelphia architect Frank Furness, original synagogue for Congregation Rodeph Shalom in 1866, though the building was torn down and replaced by the current 1928 temple building; and Pietro Belluschi, the sanctuary for Adath Israel in Merion Station in 1959.

The historic 1928 Moorish Byzantine–style synagogue of Rodeph Shalom Congregation remains in Center City, Philadelphia, and recently completed a massive restoration and renovation project. Mid-Century-Modern-, Contemporary- and Functional-style synagogues abound in the area, and a concentration of such styles can be found primarily in the suburban areas today. Synagogue architecture and style are always changing to meet the needs of the individual congregations and to showcase the new trends in design and function.

## Synagogue Architecture in Delaware and Southern New Jersey

While small in number of buildings, the synagogues and temples in Delaware reflect the same trends found in the Philadelphia area. Jewish congregations built their synagogues based on their financial and use needs and employed the current styles in fashion. The former Adas Kodesch Synagogue, located at Sixth and French Streets in Wilmington, and the former "Temple of Truth" synagogue for Congregation Beth Emeth were among the more unique and unusual houses of worship at the time they were built. Sadly, these two structures are no longer standing. When Adas Kodesch Congregation and Chesed Shel Emeth Congregation merged in 1957, they subsequently took the step of hiring Percival Goodman to design their synagogue. Mr. Goodman designed over fifty synagogues throughout the United States—more than any other single architect. The building, dedicated in 1963, reflects Goodman's use of brick and other natural elements in the design. The former Temple Beth El in Newark was built in the A-Frame style popular in the 1960s. It is the only such Jewish house of worship built in that style in the Delaware Valley.

Synagogues built in Southern New Jersey were varied both in style and size, reflecting location, wealth of the congregation and whether the congregation was primarily urban, suburban or rural, as in the case of the many synagogues found in the former Jewish farming areas outside of Camden and other larger towns in Southern New Jersey. The synagogues that were built in the Camden suburb of Cherry Hill reflect the increased growth of the congregations and also their need for large, expansive synagogue complexes to meet the religious and educational needs of the congregational membership. Today, the largest synagogue facilities can be found in the Cherry Hill area. Beth El, in western Cherry Hill, built a very large Contemporary facility in 1969. With sharp angles, modern lines and a soaring sanctuary that evokes the space age, the building appears to float. The congregation will be leaving this unique building in 2009 for its new synagogue, which is being built farther east in Vorhees. Temple Emanu-El also built a striking Contemporary temple building in eastern Cherry Hill that is many times larger than its original temple in western Cherry Hill.

The synagogues in former Jewish agricultural communities throughout Southern New Jersey often evoke the small, wooden synagogues that once existed in Poland and Eastern Europe. Many are buildings of historic stature due to design and local Jewish history. Most of these buildings are no longer used for Jewish worship, but some have been preserved in one way or another. A few are now used for Christian worship serves. The former Brotherhood Synagogue in Woodbine was a very large and elegant building constructed for the community and is now the Sam Azeez Museum of Woodbine Heritage. Some of the rural synagogues are used only occasionally for Jewish worship services. The Garten Road Synagogue–Beth Israel, built in 1890 in the community of Rosenhayn, is a wonderful example of a tiny, rural, one-room synagogue. It is the smallest of the synagogues in Southern New Jersey and opens once a year during the High Holy Days for a worship service. There are a number of efforts underway to document and preserve many of these structures.

# PHILADELPHIA-AREA SYNAGOGUES

Lower Merion Synagogue, 123 Old Lancaster Road, Bala Cynwyd, Montomgery County, Pennsylvania. Current synagogue exterior view. This Orthodox congregation was established in 1954. The current building was constructed in various stages in 1980 and the 1990s. An additional large expansion was also recently completed. Lower Merion Synagogue was one of the first Orthodox congregations in the Main Line area. *Photograph by Julian H. Preisler, 2008.*

Congregation Tifereth Israel of Lower Bucks County, 2909 Bristol Road, Bensalem, Bucks County, Pennsylvania. Current synagogue exterior view. This Conservative congregation was established in 1971 as the Neshaminy Valley Jewish Community Center. The present synagogue building was completed in 1980. *Photograph courtesy of Jeffrey J. Barnett, 2007.*

Congregation Or Shalom, 835 Darby-Paoli Road, Berwyn, Chester County, Pennsylvania. Current synagogue exterior view. This Conservative congregation was established in 1974. The original building was constructed in 1962 as a church. The synagogue complex was recently expanded and enlarged. *Photograph courtesy of Julie Miller, 2008.*

Congregation Tiferes Bet Israel, 1920 Skippack Pike, Blue Bell, Montgomery County, Pennsylvania. Current synagogue exterior view. This Conservative congregation was formed in the 1980s by the merger of Tiferes Israel of Norristown (founded 1893) and Beth Israel of Lansdale (founded pre-1971). The present synagogue was built in 1989 for the merged congregation. *Photograph by Julian H. Preisler, 1991.*

Bristol Jewish Center, Congregation Ahavath Achim, 216 Pond Street, Bristol, Bucks County, Pennsylvania. Current synagogue exterior view. This Reconstructionist congregation was established in 1904. Originally Conservative in orientation, the congregation was the first to be established in Bucks County. Its current synagogue building was constructed in 1948 and replaced an earlier structure. *Photograph courtesy of Alan J. Vogenberg, 2007.*

Congregation Beth El Ner Tamid, 715 Paxon Hollow Road, Broomall, Delaware County, Pennsylvania. Current synagogue exterior view. This Progressive Conservative congregation was established as Beth El Suburban of Broomall in 1956. It was initially sponsored by Beth El of Philadelphia, though that congregation eventually merged with Beth Hillel of Wynnewood. In 1972, the Tikvas Israel Congregation of Philadelphia merged with Beth El Suburban. In 1992, Congregation Ner Tamid of Springfield merged with Beth El, and in 2002 Temple Israel of Upper Darby, also faced with declining membership, merged with Beth El Ner Tamid. The current synagogue building is a Contemporary structure that encompassed/replaced the original synagogue built in stages in 1958, 1964 and 1972. *Photograph courtesy of Arthur Rosenthol, 2007.*

Congregation Beth El Ner Tamid, 715 Paxon Hollow Road, Broomall, Delaware County, Pennsylvania. Original synagogue exterior front view. *Photograph from the cover of the* Congregation Beth El Suburban Bar Mitzvah Year Book 1972–73. *Author's collection.*

Beth Israel Congregation, 25 South Fifth Street, Coatesville, Chester County, Pennsylvania. Former synagogue exterior side view. This Conservative congregation was originally established in 1897 as Kesher Israel. This building was constructed in 1924 and served the congregation until 1995, when the congregation dedicated a new synagogue on Pottstown Pike in Chester Spring, Upper Uwchland Township. *Photograph by Julian H. Preisler, 1991.*

Beth Israel Congregation, 25 South Fifth Street, Coatesville, Chester County, Pennsylvania. Former synagogue exterior front view. *Photograph by Julian H. Preisler, 1991.*

Temple Judea of Bucks County, 300 East Swamp Road, Doylestown, Bucks County, Pennsylvania. Current synagogue exterior view. Reform congregation. The congregation is currently in the planning stages to build a new and larger synagogue on Rogers Road. *Photograph by Julian H. Preisler, 1991.*

Temple Sinai, Limekiln Pike and Dillon Road, Dresher, Montgomery County, Dresher, Pennsylvania. Current synagogue exterior front view. This Conservative congregation was established in 1940 in Philadelphia. The current synagogue building was completed in 1978. In the mid-1980s, Congregation Ramat El-Mount Airy Jewish Community Center (founded 1951) in Philadelphia merged with the suburban Temple Sinai. *Photograph by Julian H. Preisler, 1994.*

Adath Jeshurun Congregation, 7763 Old York Road, Elkins Park, Montgomery County, Pennsylavania. Current synagogue exterior front view. This Conservative congregation was established in 1858 in Philadelphia. The present synagogue was completed in 1964. In 1989, the Tikvoh Chadashow Congregation of Mount Airy merged with Adath Jeshurun, and in 2004 the Oxford Circle Jewish Community Centre Brith Israel Congregation in Northeast Philadelphia closed and merged with Adath Jeshurun. *Photograph courtesy of Arthur Rosenthol, 2007.*

Adath Jeshurun Congregation, 7763 Old York Road, Elkins Park, Montgomery County, Pennsylavania. Current synagogue interior sanctuary view. *Photograph by Julian H. Preisler, 2008.*

Congregation Beth Sholom, 8231 Old York Road, Elkins Park, Montgomery County, Pennsylavania. Current synagogue exterior front view. This Conservative congregation was established in 1919 in the Logan section of Philadelphia. The present synagogue was completed and consecrated in 1959, and it is the only synagogue in the United States designed by world-famous architect Frank Lloyd Wright. The Beth Sholom synagogue is one of only four U.S. synagogues listed as National Historic Landmarks and one of the most recognizable synagogues in the United States. *Photograph by Julian H. Preisler, 2008.*

Congregation Beth Sholom, 8231 Old York Road, Elkins Park, Montgomery County, Pennsylavania. Current synagogue interior sanctuary view, circa 1960. *Photograph courtesy of the Jacob Rader Marcus Center of the American Jewish Archives.*

Reform Congregation Keneseth Israel, 8339 Old York Road, Elkins Park, Montgomery County, Pennsylvania. Current synagogue exterior view. This Reform congregation was established in Philadelphia in 1847. Originally Orthodox, the congregation adopted the Reform ritual in 1855 and was the only Reform congregation in Philadelphia for over forty years. The present modern synagogue was built in the 1950s. *Photograph by Julian H. Preisler, 1994.*

Reform Congregation Keneseth Israel, 8339 Old York Road, Elkins Park, Montgomery County, Pennsylvania. Current synagogue exterior front detail, circa 1950s. *Photograph courtesy of the Reform Congregation Keneseth Israel Archives.*

Congregation Kol Ami, 8201 High School Road, Elkins Park, Montgomery County, Pennsylvania. Current synagogue exterior view. This Reform congregation was established in 1994. The current building was purchased in 2006. It was originally built in the 1950s as the suburban branch of Congregation Rodef Shalom, located in Center City, Philadelphia. Rodef Shalom sold the building to concentrate activities in its Center City synagogue. *Photograph by Julian H. Preisler, 1994.*

Congregation Beth Tikvah B'nai Jeshurun, 1001 Paper Mill Road, Erdenheim, Montgomery County, Pennsylvania. Current synagogue exterior view. This Conservative congregation was established in 1973 through the merger of B'nai Jeshurun of Philadelphia (founded 1915) and Beth Tikvah of Springfield Township (founded 1956). The present synagogue was built and expanded in stages in 1958 and 1975. A major phased-in renovation and expansion was completed in 2006. *Photograph by Julian H. Preisler, 2008.*

Congregation Beth El of Lower Bucks County, 21 Penn Valley Road, Fallsington, Bucks County, Pennsylvania. Former synagogue exterior view. This Conservative congregation was formed in 1953. The Fallsington synagogue was most likely completed in the 1960s and is an excellent example of Mid-Century Modern design. The congregation, which was located near Levittown, relocated to Yardley sometime after 1991, and in 2008 it dedicated its new sanctuary and synagogue addition. *Photograph by Julian H. Preisler, 1991.*

Congregation Beth Chaim, 350 East Street Road, Featerville, Bucks County, Pennsylvania. Former synagogue exterior view. This Conservative congregation was established in 1956. The synagogue was built in stages in 1957 and 1968. The synagogue was greatly expanded with a new sanctuary sometime in the 1990s. In 2006, due to declining membership, Beth Chaim merged with Congregation Shaare Shomayim in Northeast Philadelphia. *Photograph by Julian H. Preisler, 2008.*

Beth David Reform Congregation, 1130 Vaughans Lane, Gladwyne, Montgomery County, Pennsylvania. Current synagogue exterior view. This Reform congregation was established in 1968 in the Wynnewood section of Philadelphia. *Photograph by Julian H. Preisler, 1993.*

Suburban Jewish Community Center B'nai Aaron, 560 Mill Road, Havertown, Delaware County, Pennsylvania. Current synagogue exterior detail. This Conservative congregation was formed in 1969 by the merger of B'nai Aaron of Philadelphia (founded 1926) and the Suburban Jewish Community Center Tel Or of Delaware County (founded 1951). In 1991, the Yeadon Jewish Community Center merged with SJCC-B'nai Aaron. *Photograph by Julian H. Preisler, 1994.*

Suburban Jewish Community Center B'nai Aaron, 560 Mill Road, Havertown, Delaware County, Pennsylvania. Current synagogue exterior front view. *Photograph by Arthur Rosenthol, 2007.*

Temple Brith Achim, 481 South Gulph Road, King of Prussia, Montgomery County, Pennsylvania. Current synagogue exterior view. This Reform congregation was established in 1971 as the Brotherhood Temple Brith Achim. The present synagogue was built in 1982 and expanded in 1987. *Photograph by Julian H. Preisler, 1993.*

Congregation Or Ami, 708 Ridge Pike, Lafayette Hill, Montgomery County, Pennsylvania. Current synagogue exterior view. This Reform congregation was established in 1947 in the Roxborough section of Philadelphia as the Jewish Community Group of Roxborough. Originally Conservative, the congregation relocated to Lafayette Hill in 1960 and became known as the Ivy Ridge Jewish Community Center. The present building was constructed in 1960 and was expanded and remodeled in 1964, 1972 and 1990. *Photograph by Julian H. Preisler, 2008.*

Beth Israel Congregation, 1080 Sumneytown Pike, Lansdale, Montgomery County, Pennsylvania. Exterior view of former building, 1971. This Conservative congregation was established prior to 1971 and merged with Norristown's Tiferes Israel in the 1980s to become Tiferet Bet Israel of Blue Bell. *Photograph from the cover of the* Synagogue Dedication Booklet, 1971/5731. *Author's collection.*

Temple Shalom, 2901 Edgely Road, Levittown, Bucks County, Pennsylvania. Current synagogue exterior view. This Reform congregation was established in 1953. *Photograph by Julian H. Preisler, 1993.*

Beth Chaim Reform Congregation, 389 Conestoga Road, Malvern, Chester County, Pennsylvania. Current synagogue exterior view. This Reform congregation was founded in 1992. The present synagogue building was dedicated in 2007. *Photograph courtesy of Len Shyles, 2007.*

Beth Chaim Reform Congregation, 389 Conestoga Road, Malvern, Chester County, Pennsylvania. Current synagogue sanctuary interior view. *Photograph courtesy of Len Shyles, 2007.*

Congregation Beth Or, 239 Welsh Road, Maple Glen, Montgomery County, Pennsylvania. Current synagogue exterior view. This Reform congregation was established in 1954 in Northwest Philadelphia. The present synagogue was dedicated in 2006, when the congregation relocated from Spring House. *Photograph by Julian H. Preisler, 2008.*

Melrose B'nai Israel Emanu-El Congregation, 133 Cheltenham Avenue, Melrose Park, Montgomery County, Pennsylvania. Current synagogue exterior view. This Conservative congregation was established in 1957 through the merger of the B'nai Israel Congregation of Olney in Philadelphia and the Melrose Congregation of suburban Cheltenham. In 1985, Emanu-El Congregation of Philadelphia joined to form the present-day congregation. The synagogue building was constructed in 1959. *Photograph by Julian H. Preisler, 2008.*

Adath Israel Congregation, 250 North Highland Avenue, Merion Station, Montgomery County, Pennsylvania. Current synagogue exterior view. This Conservative congregation was formed in 1946. The present synagogue was built in 1953 and 1959, when the sanctuary designed by well-known architect Pietro Belluschi was completed. In 2006, Beth T'fillah of Overbrook in Philadelphia merged with Adath Israel. *Photograph courtesy of Arthur Rosenthol, 2007.*

Adath Israel Congregation, 250 North Highland Avenue, Merion Station, Montgomery County, Pennsylvania. Original synagogue exterior view. *Photograph by Julian H. Preisler, 1993.*

Sir Ami Bucks County Jewish Congregation, 101 Richboro Road, Newtown, Bucks County, Pennsylvania. Current synagogue exterior view. This Reform congregation was established in 1976. The present synagogue was built in 1980 and 1988. *Photograph by Julian H. Preisler, 1992.*

Tiferes Israel Congregation, 1541 Powell Street, Norristown, Montgomery County, Pennsylvania. Former synagogue exterior view. Established in 1893, this Conservative congregation merged with Beth Israel of Lansdale in the 1980s and formed a new congregation, Tiferet Bet Israel. A new synagogue was built in 1989 in suburban Blue Bell. The former Norristown synagogue was built in 1948, and a large addition was constructed in 1969. *Photograph by Julian H. Preisler, 2008.*

Beth Am Israel Congregation, 1301 Hagys Ford Road, Penn Valley, Montgomery County, Pennsylvania. Current synagogue exterior view. This Conservative congregation was established in 1924 in Southwest Philadelphia. The present synagogue was dedicated in 2003. *Photograph courtesy of Arthur Rosenthol, 2007.*

Beth Am Israel Congregation, 1301 Hagys Ford Road, Penn Valley, Montgomery County, Pennsylvania. Former synagogue exterior view. This building was constructed in 1968 and was replaced, on the same site, by the current 2003 building. *Photograph by Julian H. Preisler, 1992.*

Har Zion Temple, 1500 Hagys Ford Road, Penn Valley, Montgomery County, Pennsylvania. Current synagogue exterior view. This Conservative congregation was established in the Wynnefield section of Philadelphia in 1923. The present synagogue was completed in 1976. *Photograph by Julian H. Preisler, 1992.*

Adath Jeshurun Congregation, Seventh Street and Cecil B. Moore Avenue, Philadelphia, Pennsylvania. Former synagogue exterior view. This was the first purpose-built synagogue for the Conservative congregation, which was established in 1858. The cornerstone of this former synagogue was laid in 1886. The congregation built a new synagogue in 1912 at Broad and Diamond Streets and then, in 1964, relocated to suburban Elkins Park. *Photograph by Julian H. Preisler, 2008.*

Adath Jeshurun Congregation, North Broad and Diamond Streets, Philadelphia, Pennsylvania. Former synagogue exterior view, undated. This synagogue was built in 1912 and enlarged in 1926. The building no longer stands. *Photograph courtesy of Adath Jeshurun Congregation Archives and Gavi Miller.*

*Right*: Adath Jeshurun Congregation, North Broad and Diamond Streets, Philadelphia, Pennsylvania. Former synagogue sanctuary interior view, undated. *Photograph courtesy of Adath Jeshurun Congregation Archives and Gavi Miller.*

*Below*: Adath Shalom Congregation, South Marshall and Ritner Streets, Philadelphia, Pennsylvania. Synagogue exterior view. This Conservative congregation in South Philadelphia was formed in 1950 by the merger of Shaare Israel, Beth Samuel and B'nai Moshe. The building dates to either 1922 or 1930, when Beth Samuel was established, but it is not known if it was built as a synagogue. Originally Orthodox, the congregation became Conservative in 1950 upon the merger of the three groups. The synagogue closed sometime after 2005, but it is not known whether the congregation merged with another congregation or disbanded. *Photograph by Julian H. Preisler, 1995.*

Adath Tikvah Monefiore Congregation, Summerdale and Hoffnagle Streets, Philadelphia, Pennsylvania. Former synagogue exterior view. This Conservative congregation in Northeast Philadelphia was established prior to 1953, when the former synagogue was built. In 2003, the congregation merged with Ohev Shalom in Richboro, Bucks County. The former synagogue is now home to Stern Hebrew High School. *Photograph by Julian H. Preisler, 1995.*

Adath Zion Congregation, Pennway and Friendship Streets, Philadelphia, Pennsylvania. Former synagogue exterior view. This Conservative congregation located in the Oxford Circle section of Northeast Philadelphia was established in 1893 in the Frankford section of Philadelphia. The synagogue in Oxford Circle was built in 1956. In 2008, Adath Zion closed and merged with a nearby congregation, Ner Zedek Ezrath Israel Beth Uziel. *Photograph by Julian H. Preisler, 2008.*

*Right*: Adath Zion Congregation, Pennway and Friendship Streets, Philadelphia, Pennsylvania. Former synagogue exterior detail. *Photograph by Arthur Rosenthol, 2007.*

*Below*: Ahavath Israel of Oak Lane, North Sixth Street, Philadelphia, Pennsylvania. Former synagogue exterior view. This Orthodox congregation was established in 1927. The unusual International-style modern synagogue, designed by noted architect Louis I. Kahn, was completed in 1937. The congregation closed in 1981. *Photograph by Julian H. Preisler, 2008.*

Beth Am Israel Congregation, 5747 Warrington Avenue, Philadelphia, Pennsylvania. Former synagogue exterior view, undated. This Conservative congregation in Southwest Philadelphia was founded in 1922 and chartered in 1924. The synagogue was completed in 1926. In the late 1960s, the congregation relocated to suburban Penn Valley. *Photograph courtesy of Beth Am Israel Congregation Archives.*

Temple Beth El—The Rothschild Synagogue, Fifty-eighth and Walnut Streets, Philadelphia, Pennsylvania. Former synagogue exterior view. This Conservative congregation was established in West Philadelphia in 1907. The synagogue was built in 1915, and a community center was added in 1922. The architect was Louis Levi. Funded by Philadelphia businessman Edward Rothschild, the synagogue was dedicated to the memory of his parents. Later remodeled and expanded, it was rededicated to the memory of Edward Rothschild. In 1970, Beth El merged with Beth Hillel in suburban Wynnewood to become Congregation Beth Hillel Beth El. *Photograph courtesy of Brian Decker, 2007.*

Congregation Beth Emeth B'nai Yitzchok, Bustleton and Unruh Avenues, Philadelphia, Pennsylvania. Former synagogue exterior view. This Conservative congregation was located in Northeast Philadelphia. Beth Emeth was established in 1950, and B'nai Yitzchok was established in 1924. The two congregations merged in 1989 and held services in the Beth Emeth synagogue built in 1959. In 2007, the synagogue closed and merged with Congregation Shaare Shomayim in Northeast Philadelphia. *Photograph by Julian H. Preisler, 1990.*

Congregation Beth Hamedrosh, 7505 Brookhaven Road, Philadelphia, Pennsylvania. Former synagogue exterior view. This Conservative congregation in the Overbrook section of West Philadelphia was established in the 1950s. The synagogue was built in 1960–61. The congregation purchased land in suburban Wynnewood in 2000 and relocated to a newly built synagogue in 2007. The former synagogue in Overbrook is now home to a congregation of African American Hebrew Israelites. *Photograph by Julian H. Preisler, 1990.*

Congregation Beth Hamedrosh, 7505 Brookhaven Road, Philadelphia, Pennsylvania. Former synagogue present exterior view. *Photograph by Julian H. Preisler, 2008.*

Congregation Beth Israel, Thirty-second Street and Montgomery Avenue, Philadelphia, Pennsylvania. Former synagogue exterior side view. First established in 1840 as Philadelphia's first Conservative congregation, the synagogue in the Strawberry Mansion section of Philadelphia was built in either 1907 or 1924. In 1964, the congregation merged with Beth Zion in Center City, Philadelphia, to become Temple Beth Zion–Beth Israel. *Photograph by Julian H. Preisler, 2008.*

Congregation Beth Israel, Thirty-second Street and Montgomery Avenue, Philadelphia, Pennsylvania. Former synagogue exterior front view. *Photograph by Julian H. Preisler, 1990.*

Congregation Beth Jacob, 6027–29 Chestnut Street, Philadelphia, Pennsylvania. Former synagogue exterior front view. Established in 1914, the congregation's synagogue was built in 1947. Sources indicate a 1922 building, but it is not known if that building was on this same site. Beth Jacob closed in the early 1960s and merged with Beth Hamedrash Hagadol, located at the time at Sixtieth and Larchwood Streets in West Philadelphia. *Photograph by Julian H. Preisler, 1992.*

Congregation Beth Judah, 5426 Sansom Street, Philadelphia, Pennsylvania. Former synagogue exterior view. This Orthodox congregation was established in 1905 and chartered in 1908. Originally known as the Hebrew Congregation of West Philadelphia, the congregation disbanded in 1968 and the building was sold. *Photograph by Julian H. Preisler, 1992.*

Beth Sholom Congregation, North Broad and Courtland Streets, Philadelphia, Pennsylvania. Former synagogue current exterior view. This Conservative congregation was established in 1917 as the Logan Congregation Ahavas Israel. Chartered in 1919, the name was changed to Beth Sholom. The Broad Street synagogue was built in 1922, and the architect was Jacob Ethan Fieldstein. In the 1940s, a school and center were established in suburban Elkins Park. The congregation relocated completely to Elkins Park when their Frank Lloyd Wright–designed synagogue was completed in 1959. *Photograph by Julian H. Preisler, 2008.*

Beth Sholom Congregation, North Broad and Courtland Streets, Philadelphia, Pennsylvania. Former synagogue exterior view, 1951. *Photograph courtesy of PhillyHistory.org, a project of the Philadelphia Department of Records.*

Congregation Beth Solomon Community Center, 198 Tomlinson Road, Philadelphia, Pennsylvania. Current synagogue exterior front view. This Orthodox congregation was established in the 1960s in Northeast Philadelphia. The current synagogue was built in 2000. *Photograph courtesy of Arthur Rosenthol, 2007.*

Congregation Beth T'Fillah, 7630 Woodbine Avenue, Philadelphia, Pennsylvania. Former synagogue exterior view. This Conservative congregation in the Overbrook section of West Philadelphia was established in 1948 as the Overbrook Park Synagogue. The synagogue was built in 1951. In 2006, Beth T'fillah closed and merged with Adath Israel in nearby Merion Station. *Photograph by Julian H. Preisler, 2008.*

Congregation Beth Tefilath Israel Rodeph Zedek (BTIRZ) of Pennypack Park, 2605 Welsh Road, Philadelphia, Pennsylvania. Former synagogue exterior view. This Conservative congregation was composed of several earlier congregations. The two main congregations, Beth Tefilath Israel (founded 1910) and Rodeph Zedek (founded 1953), merged in 1982. The Welsh Road synagogue was built circa 1951. BTIRZ closed in 1998 and merged with Congregation Shaare Shomayim in the Far Northeast section of Philadelphia. *Photograph by Julian H. Preisler, 1990.*

Temple Beth Torah, 608 Welsh Road, Philadelphia, Pennsylvania. Former synagogue exterior front view. Established in 1949 as the first Reform congregation in Northeast Philadelphia, Beth Torah was chartered in 1950 as the Boulevard Temple. The synagogue was built in 1963 or 1965. In 2004, Beth Torah closed and merged with Old York Road Temple–Beth Ami in suburban Elkins Park. *Photograph by Julian H. Preisler, 1992.*

Beth Tovim Congregtion, 5871 Drexel Road, Philadelphia, Pennsylvania. Current synagogue exterior view. This Orthodox congregation in the Wynnefield section of West Philadelphia was established in 1964. It was named for its benefactor, Tuvia, who purchased a former mansion for use as the synagogue. *Photograph by Julian H. Preisler, 2008.*

Beth Uziel Congregation, Rorer Street and Wyoming Avenue, Philadelphia, Pennsylvania. Former synagogue exterior view, right side. This Conservative congregation in the Feltonville section of Philadelphia was established in 1943. The synagogue was dedicated in 1954. In 1994, the congregation closed and merged with Ner Zedek Ezrath Israel in Northeast Philadelphia. *Photograph by Julian H. Preisler, 1993.*

Beth Uziel Congregation, Rorer Street and Wyoming Avenue, Philadelphia, Pennsylvania. Former synagogue exterior view, left side. *Photograph by Julian H. Preisler, 1993.*

Temple Beth Zion Beth Israel Neziner, 300 South Eighteenth Street, Philadelphia, Pennsylvania. Current synagogue exterior view. This Conservative congregation is located in Center City, Philadelphia. The present-day congregation was established through the merger, circa 1964, of Beth Zion (founded 1946) and Beth Israel (founded 1840). The current synagogue building, originally built as a church in 1894, was purchased and remodeled in 1954. The remodel was designed by Beryl Price. The former Neziner Congregation, established in 1887, merged with Beth Zion Beth Israel in 1983. *Photograph courtesy of Arthur Rosenthol, 2007.*

B'nai Aaron Congregation, Fifty-third and Euclid Streets, Philadelphia, Pennsylvania. Former synagogue exterior view. This Conservative synagogue and community center located in the Wynnefield section of West Philadelphia was established in 1926. The synagogue was built in 1949 and designed by Louis Magaziner. The synagogue has a stark modern exterior, but an ornate interior. B'nai Aaron closed and merged with the Suburban Jewish Community Center (SJCC) in Havertown in 1969 to form SJCC-B'nai Aaron. *Photograph courtesy of Arthur Rosenthol, 2007.*

Congregation B'nai Abraham, 521–27 Lombard Street, Philadelphia, Pennsylvania. Current synagogue exterior view. This Orthodox congregation located in the Center City area of Philadelphia was established in 1882. The current building was constructed in 1910. It is one of the earliest large, Eastern European synagogues established in the area that was considered the original Jewish Quarter of Philadelphia. The synagogue has undergone renovation and restoration projects over the last few years in an attempt to restore the building to its former glory. *Photograph by Julian H. Preisler, 2008.*

Congregation B'nai Halberstam, 610 North Sixth Street, Philadelphia, Pennsylvania. Former synagogue exterior view. This Orthodox congregation was established in 1886. The synagogue, a former church, was purchased in 1891 and remodeled for use by the Jewish congregation. Through a variety of mergers and moves during the 1960s and later, the congregation has been part of B'nai Israel Ohev Zedek in Northeast Philadelphia since the late 1970s. *Photograph by Julian H. Preisler, 2008.*

Congregation B'nai Israel Ohev Zedek B'nai Halberstam, 8201 Castor Avenue, Philadelphia, Pennsylvania. Current synagogue exterior view. This Orthodox congregation in Northeast Philadelphia was formed through a merger of many once-separate Orthodox congregations. Among them are Ohev Zedek, B'nai Israel, B'nai Halberstam and Anshe Emeth, most of which were established in the late nineteenth century. The Mount Airy Orthodox Congregation merged into the B'nai Israel Ohev Zedek group in 1958. The merged congregation relocated to the Northeast area in the 1970s and built the present synagogue in the 1980s. *Photograph by Arthur Rosenthol, 2007.*

B'nai Jacob–Dirshu Tov Congregation, 1147 Gillham Street, Philadelphia, Pennsylvania. Current synagogue exterior view. This Orthodox congregation was established in the early 1960s by the merger of B'nai Jacob (founded 1913 in Strawberry Mansion) and Dirshu Tov (founded 1891 in Northern Liberties). The present synagogue, a remodeled home in Northeast Philadelphia, was occupied when the merger took place circa 1962. *Photograph by Julian H. Preisler, 1992.*

Congregation B'nai Jeshurun, Thirty-third and Diamond Streets, Philadelphia, Pennsylvania. Former synagogue exterior view. This Conservative congregation in the Strawberry Mansion section of Philadelphia was established in 1915. The synagogue was dedicated in 1925. By the 1950s, the congregation merged with Adath Shalom of Mount Airy, and by the early 1960s the combined congregation merged with the disbanded Ahavas Chesed of Germantown and used its building. The renamed congregation, B'nai Jeshurun–Ahavas Chesed, merged with Beth Tikvah of suburban Erdenheim in the early 1970s. *Photograph by Julian H. Preisler, 2008.*

Congregation B'nai Moshe Anshe Sfard, 1711 South Fifth Street, Philadelphia, Pennsylvania. Former synagogue exterior view, undated. This Orthodox congregation in South Philadelphia was established in 1903. The synagogue was built in 1904 and altered in 1938. Poale Zedek, which was a merged congregation of several other Orthodox congregations, merged with B'nai Moshe in the early 1960s. Congregation B'nai Moshe Anshe Sfard closed in the early 1980s. *Photograph courtesy of the Philadelphia Jewish Archives Center.*

Congregation B'nai Reuben Anshe Sfard, 615 South Sixth Street, Philadelphia, Pennsylvania. Former synagogue exterior side view. This Orthodox congregation in South Philadelphia was established in 1883 and chartered in 1888. The synagogue was built circa 1904. By the 1950s, the congregation had disbanded, and since then the building has been used for commercial purposes. Today, the building is an antique store. *Photograph by Julian H. Preisler, 2008.*

Congregation B'nai Reuben Anshe Sfard, 615 South Sixth Street, Philadelphia, Pennsylvania. Former synagogue exterior front view. *Photograph by Julian H. Preisler, 2008.*

Congregation B'nai Yitzchok, 243 East Roosevelt Boulevard, Philadelphia, Pennsylvania. Former synagogue exterior front view. This Conservative congregation in the Feltonville section of Northeast Philadelphia was established in 1924. The synagogue was built between 1948 and 1951. B'nai Yitzchok merged with Congregation Beth Emeth in 1989 and relocated to the Beth Emeth synagogue on Bustleton Avenue. Beth Emeth B'nai Yitzchok closed in 2007 and merged with Congregation Shaare Shomayim, located in the Far Northeast section of Philadelphia. *Photograph by Julian H. Preisler, 2008.*

Congregation B'nai Yitzchok, 243 East Roosevelt Boulevard, Philadelphia, Pennsylvania. Former synagogue exterior detail view. *Photograph by Julian H. Preisler, 1992.*

Brith Israel Congregation, D Street and East Roosevelt Boulevard, Philadelphia, Pennsylvania. Former synagogue exterior front view. This Conservative congregation was established in 1922 in the Feltonville section of Northeast Philadelphia. The synagogue was built in 1930 and designed by architect David Supowitz. An addition was completed in the 1940s. In 1990, the congregation closed and merged with the Oxford Circle Jewish Community Centre (OCJCC). The merged congregation, OCJCC–Brith Israel, closed in 2004 and merged with Adath Jeshurun in suburban Elkins Park. *Photograph by Julian H. Preisler, 2008.*

Brith Israel Congregation, D Street and East Roosevelt Boulevard, Philadelphia, Pennsylvania. Former synagogue exterior front detail. *Photograph by Julian H. Preisler, 1990.*

Emanu-El Congregation, Stenton Avenue and Old York Road, Philadelphia, Pennsylvania. Former synagogue exterior view. This Conservative congregation is thought to have been established in 1925. The synagogue, in the Oak Lane area of Philadelphia, was built between 1946 and 1951. In 1985, Emanu-El merged with Melrose B'nai Israel in Cheltenham and sold the Stenton Avenue synagogue. *Photograph by Julian H. Preisler, 2008.*

Emanu-El Congregation, Stenton Avenue and Old York Road, Philadelphia, Pennsylvania. Former synagogue exterior view, circa 1950. *Photograph courtesy of the Philadelphia Jewish Archives Center, from a synagogue membership brochure, 1950s.*

Chevra Emunas Israel Ohev Sholom Congregation, Fifth and Gaskill Streets, Philadelphia, Pennsylvania. Former synagogue exterior view, 1959. This Orthodox congregation was established in 1881 as Emunas Israel. Ohev Sholom merged with Emunas Israel in 1887. The synagogue, located in the Society Hill section of Center City, Philadelphia, was originally the Garrick Theatre. The building was remodeled as a synagogue and dedicated in 1891. Also known as the Hungarian Synagogue, the congregation closed by the late 1960s, and the synagogue building was later torn down. *Photograph courtesy of PhillyHistory.org, a project of the Philadelphia Department of Records.*

Henry S. Frank Memorial Synagogue, 5400 Old York Road, Philadelphia, Pennsylvania. Synagogue exterior angle view. Located on the grounds of the Einstein Medical Center (former Jewish Hospital of Philadelphia) in North Philadelphia, the synagogue, built in 1901, is now used for special occasions and was recently restored. It is a Registered Historical Landmark and was designed by the noted architect Arnold W. Brunner, one of the first American-born Jewish architects. *Photograph by Julian H. Preisler, 1990.*

Henry S. Frank Memorial Synagogue, 5400 Old York Road, Philadelphia, Pennsylvania. Vintage synagogue exterior view, circa 1905. *Photograph courtesy of PhillyHistory.org, a project of the Philadelphia Department of Records.*

Germantown Jewish Centre, 400 West Ellet Street at Lincoln Drive, Philadelphia, Pennsylvania. Current synagogue exterior entrance view. This Conservative/Renewal congregation is located in the Mount Airy section of Northwest Philadelphia. Established in 1936, the present synagogue was built in 1947, and the large sanctuary was dedicated in 1954. *Photograph by Julian H. Preisler, 1994.*

Germantown Jewish Centre, 400 West Ellet Street at Lincoln Drive, Philadelphia, Pennsylvania. Current synagogue exterior view. *Photograph by Julian H. Preisler, 2008.*

Har Zion Temple, Fifty-fourth Street and Wynnefield Avenue, Philadelphia, Pennsylvania. Former synagogue exterior view. This Conservative congregation in the Wynnefield section of West Philadelphia was established in 1923. The synagogue was built in 1924 and was one of the largest in the Wynnefield area. In 1976, the congregation dedicated its new synagogue in suburban Penn Valley. *Photograph by Julian H. Preisler, 2008.*

Temple Israel of Wynnefield, Fifty-ninth Street and Woodbine Avenue, Philadelphia, Pennsylvania. Former synagogue exterior view. This Conservative congregation located in the Wynnefield section of West Philadelphia was founded in 1943. The synagogue was built in 1953. In 1985, the congregation merged with Adath Israel, located nearby in suburban Merion Station. *Photograph by Julian H. Preisler, 2008.*

Temple Judea, 6929 North Broad Street, Philadelphia, Pennsylvania. Former synagogue exterior view. This Reform congregation in the East Oak Lane neighborhood of Philadelphia was established in 1928. The unusual Colonial-style synagogue was built in 1939. In 1982, Temple Judea closed and merged with Reform Congregation Keneseth Israel in suburban Elkins Park. *Photograph by Julian H. Preisler, 2008.*

Temple Judea, 6929 North Broad Street, Philadelphia, Pennsylvania. Former synagogue exterior drawing, 1950s. *Image courtesy of Reform Congregation Keneseth Israel Archives.*

Keneses Israel Anshe Afard, 984 North Marshall Street, Philadelphia, Pennsylvania. Former synagogue exterior view. This Orthodox congregation was established in 1908 in the Northern Liberties area of North Philadelphia. The synagogue, a former church, was purchased and remodeled in 1911. By the 1960s, the congregation relocated to Northeast Philadelphia. The congregation no longer exists. *Photograph by Julian H. Preisler, 2008.*

Reform Congregation Keneseth Israel, Sixth and Brown Streets, Philadelphia, Pennsylvania. Former synagogue exterior drawing, undated. This was the first synagogue building purposely constructed for the congregation. It was dedicated in 1864. The building is no longer standing. *Image courtesy of Reform Congregation Keneseth Israel Archives.*

Reform Congregation Keneseth Israel, 1717 North Broad Street, Philadelphia, Pennsylvania. Former synagogue exterior view. This Reform congregation was formed in 1847 and is now located in suburban Elkins Park. The Broad Street temple, constructed in 1915, was destroyed by fire in the 1960s, and all that remained was the former Alumni Building. It is now named "Rock Hall" and is used by the Temple University School of Music. *Photograph by Julian H. Preisler, 1994.*

Reform Congregation Keneseth Israel, 1717 North Broad Street, Philadelphia, Pennsylvania. Former synagogue chapel interior view, undated. *Photograph courtesy of Reform Congregation Keneseth Israel Archives.*

Reform Congregation Keneseth Israel, 1717 North Broad Street, Philadelphia, Pennsylvania. Former synagogue exterior view, circa 1915. *Photograph courtesy of Reform Congregation Keneseth Israel Archives.*

Reform Congregation Keneseth Israel, 1717 North Broad Street, Philadelphia, Pennsylvania. Former synagogue sanctuary interior view, 1905. *Photograph courtesy of Reform Congregation Keneseth Israel Archives.*

Reform Congregation Keneseth Israel, 1717 North Broad Street, Philadelphia, Pennsylvania. Former synagogue remodeled sanctuary interior view, 1937. *Photograph courtesy of Reform Congregation Keneseth Israel Archives.*

Kesher Israel Congregation, 412 Lombard Street, Philadelphia, Pennsylvania. Current synagogue exterior view. This Orthodox congregation is located in the Society Hill section of Center City, Philadelphia. Established in 1893, the synagogue is a former church that was originally built about 1796. By 1887, it had become a synagogue, and Kesher Israel began using the building around 1894. The historic structure was remodelled and restored beginning in 1998. *Photograph by Julian H. Preisler, 2008.*

Temple Menorah Keneseth Chai, 4301 Tyson Avenue, Philadelphia, Pennsylvania. Current synagogue sanctuary exterior view. This Conservative congregation in Northeast Philadelphia was established in 1924 as the Tacony Hebrew Congregation. Its name was later changed to the Northeast Jewish Community Center and then Temple Menorah. The current synagogue sacntuary was built in 1951–52. In 1987, the Reform congregation Keneseth Chai of Fox Chase (founded 1982) merged with Temple Menorah to form the present congregation. *Photograph by Julian H. Preisler, 2008.*

Temple Menorah Keneseth Chai, 4301 Tyson Avenue, Philadelphia, Pennsylvania. Original synagogue exterior view. *Photograph by Julian H. Preisler, 1994.*

Mikveh Israel Congregation, North Broad and West York Streets, Philadelphia, Pennsylvania. Former synagogue exterior view. This Orthodox congregation was the first Jewish congregation established, in 1740, in Pennsylvania. Also known as Kahal Kadosh Mikveh Israel, the congregation's Broad Street synagogue was dedicated in 1909 and designed by the architectural firm of Pilcher and Tachau. The synagogue relocated in 1976 to Independence Mall East, and the Broad Street complex was used for a time as Dropsie College and Gratz College. *Photograph by Julian H. Preisler, 2008.*

Mikveh Israel Congregation, 44 North Fourth Street, Philadelphia, Pennsylvania. Current synagogue exterior view. The current synagogue, located in Center City at Independence Mall East, was dedicated in 1976 and designed by noted architect Louis I. Kahn. *Photograph by Julian H. Preisler, 1994.*

Mikveh Israel Congregation, North Broad and West York Streets, Philadelphia, Pennsylvania. Former synagogue exterior view, 1925. *Photograph courtesy of PhillyHistory.org, a project of the Philadelphia Department of Records.*

Mikveh Israel Congregation, Seventh and North Arch Streets, Philadelphia, Pennsylvania. Former synagogue interior view, undated. This synagogue was built in 1860 and was the third synagogue constructed by the congregation. The building is no longer standing. *Photograph courtesy of the Jacob Rader Marcus Center of the American Jewish Archives.*

Congregation Ner Zedek Ezrath Israel Beth Uziel, Oakmont Street and Bustleton Avenue, Philadelphia, Pennsylvania. Current synagogue exterior view. This Conservative congregation in Northeast Philadelphia is composed of several earlier congregations. Boulevard Park Jewish Congregation and Brith Kodesh Congregation merged in 1960 to form Ner Zedek Congregation. Ezrath Israel Congregation joined in 1970, and Beth Uziel Congregation joined in 1995 to form the present-day congregation. The synagogue was built in either 1964 or 1969, originally for the Ner Zedek Congregation. *Photograph by Julian H. Preisler, 2008.*

Neziner Congregation, 771 South Second Street, Philadelphia, Pennsylvania. Former synagogue exterior view, circa 1930s. This Conservative congregation in South Philadelphia was established in 1887. In 1906, the congregation purchased a former church building. The Neziner Congregation merged with Temple Beth Zion Beth Israel in 1983. The building later became a condominium. *Photograph courtesy of the Philadelphia Jewish Archives Center.*

Congregation Ohev Zedek, Mount Pleasant and Woolston Avenues, Philadelphia, Pennsylvania. Former synagogue exterior view. This Orthodox congregation comprises several earlier congregations going back to 1889. It was also known as the Mount Airy Orthodox Congregation. The synagogue building in the Mount Airy/West Oak Lane section of Philadelphia was completed circa 1960. The congregation merged again with several smaller congregations and became known as B'nai Israel Ohev Zedek. It relocated to Northeast Philadelphia and built a new synagogue circa 1980. *Photograph by Julian H. Preisler, 2008.*

Oxford Circle Jewish Community Centre, 1009 Unruh Avenue, Philadelphia, Pennsylvania. Former synagogue exterior view. This Conservative congregation was formed in 1948. The large sanctuary was built in 1963. Oxford Circle Jewish Community Centre and Brith Israel merged in 1990, and they used the Oxford Circle synagogue until 2004, when they merged with Adath Jeshurun Congregation in suburban Elkins Park. *Photograph by Julian H. Preisler, 2008.*

Oxford Circle Jewish Community Centre, 1009 Unruh Avenue, Philadelphia, Pennsylvania. Former synagogue sanctuary interior view, circa 1963. *Photograph courtesy of Adath Jeshurun Congregation Archives and Gavi Miller.*

Oxford Circle Jewish Community Centre, 1009 Unruh Avenue, Philadelphia, Pennsylvania. Original synagogue exterior view, circa 1950s. *Photograph courtesy of Adath Jeshurun Congregation Archives and Gavi Miller.*

Ramat El Congregation–Mount Airy Jewish Community Center, Johnson and Ardleigh Streets, Philadelphia, Pennsylvania. Former synagogue present exterior view. This Conservative congregation was located in the Mount Airy/West Oak Lane section of Philadelphia. The congregation was established in 1951, and the synagogue was built in stages over the years from 1951 to 1964. In 1984, Ramat El merged with Temple Sinai in suburban Dresher. *Photograph by Julian H. Preisler, 2008.*

Ramat El Congregation–Mount Airy Jewish Community Center, Johnson and Ardleigh Streets, Philadelphia, Pennsylvania. Former synagogue exterior sanctuary view. *Photograph by Julian H. Preisler, 1994.*

Congregation Shaarey Yitzchok, 2033 East Allegheny Avenue, Kensington section, Philadelphia, Pennsylvania. Former synagogue exterior view. Established in 1920, the row house–style synagogue was built in 1924. The congregation disbanded in 1990. Originally Orthodox, the congregation later became Conservative. *Photograph courtesy of Arthur Rosenthol, 2007.*

*Above*: Rodeph Shalom Congregation, 615 North Broad Street, Philadelphia, Pennsylvania. Current synagogue sanctuary interior view, undated. This Reform congregation was established in 1795. It was the first Ashkenazic congregation formed in the Western Hemisphere. Originally Orthodox, the congregation became Reform and was a charter member of the Union of American Hebrew Congregations. The landmark synagogue was built in 1926–28 and is located just north of Center City, Philadelphia. *Photograph by Jules Schick and courtesy of the Jacob Rader Marcus Center of the American Jewish Archives.*

*Left*: Rodeph Shalom Congregation, 615 North Broad Street, Philadelphia, Pennsylvania. Former synagogue exterior view, undated. The Moorish-style synagogue was built in 1866 and designed by noted Philadelphia architect Frank Furness. The building was torn down to make way for the current synagogue, which was built in 1928. *Photograph courtesy of the Jacob Rader Marcus Center of the American Jewish Archives.*

Rodeph Shalom Congregation, 615 North Broad Street, Philadelphia, Pennsylvania. Current synagogue exterior side view. *Photograph courtesy of Arthur Rosenthol, 2007.*

Rodeph Shalom Congregation, 615 North Broad Street, Philadelphia, Pennsylvania. Current synagogue exterior front view. Additions were made in 1957 and 1966. The congregation recently completed a multimillion-dollar restoration and renovation project. *Photograph courtesy of Arthur Rosenthol, 2007.*

Congregations of Shaare Shamayim, 9768 Verree Road, Philadelphia, Pennsylvania. Current synagogue sanctuary exterior view. The traditional congregation located in Northeast Philadelphia was established in 1962 as the Greater Northeast Jewish Congregation. In 1967, the original Shaare Shamyim Congregation in Philadelphia (founded 1907) merged with the suburban congregation. The synagogue was built in 1963 and 1968, and a new large sanctuary was dedicated in 1971. As various Conservative and Traditional congregations have closed in other neighborhoods of Northeast Philadelphia, a large number have merged with Shaare Shamayim, including Beth Judah, Beth Tefilath Israel–Rodef Zedek, Beth Chaim and Beth Emeth–B'nai Yitzchok. The name of the congregation was changed to the Congregations of Shaare Shamayim to reflect the various entities that are now part of the single unified congregation. *Photograph by Julian H. Preisler, 2008.*

Congregations of Shaare Shamayim, 9768 Verree Road, Philadelphia, Pennsylvania. Current synagogue original building view. *Photograph by Julian H. Preisler, 1994.*

*Right*: Temple Sholom, Large Street and Roosevelt Boulevard, Philadelphia, Pennsylvania. Former synagogue front view. This Conservative congregation in Northeast Philadelphia was established in 1940. The Colonial-style synagogue was built in 1942 and rebuilt in 1991 after a fire. The congregation closed prior to 2008 and merged with Beth Sholom Congregation in suburban Elkins Park. *Photograph by Julian H. Preisler, 1994.*

*Below*: Temple Sholom, Large Street and Roosevelt Boulevard, Philadelphia, Pennsylvania. Former synagogue exterior view. *Photograph by Julian H. Preisler, 2008.*

Temple Sinai, Washington Avenue and Limekiln Pike, Philadelphia, Pennsylvania. Former synagogue exterior front view. This Conservative congregation was established in 1940. The synagogue was built in 1948–51 and designed by Herman Ploss. A suburban school facility in Dresher was built in 1971, and complete relocation to suburban Dresher occurred in 1979 with the dedication of the current synagogue. *Photograph by Julian H. Preisler, 1994.*

Temple Sinai, Washington Avenue and Limekiln Pike, Philadelphia, Pennsylvania. Former synagogue exterior view. *Photograph by Julian H. Preisler, 2008.*

Society Hill Synagogue, 418 Spruce Street, Philadelphia, Pennsylvania. Current synagogue interior view. This unaffiliated Progressive congregation was formed in the mid-1960s. It acquired the present synagogue in 1967. Originally built as a church in 1829, the building became home, in 1910, to Congregation Beth Hamedrosh Hagadol Nusach Ashkenaz, also known as the Great Roumanian Shul. The building, which is in the Society Hill section of Center City, Philadelphia, has been restored and renovated over the years. A large-scale fundraising campaign began in 2008 for additional renovations to the existing synagogue and for expansion into an adjacent building for use as classrooms, offices and a music room. *Photograph courtesy of Todd Halpern, 2007.*

Society Hill Synagogue, 418 Spruce Street, Philadelphia, Pennsylvania. Synagogue exterior view, 1959. *Photograph courtesy of PhillyHistory.org, a project of the Philadelphia Department of Records.*

Sons of Jacob Congregation, 418 Lombard Street, Philadelphia, Pennsylvania. Former synagogue exterior view, circa 1890. This Orthodox congregation was established in 1883. The synagogue was originally built as a church. The Sons of Jacob Congregation combined with Anshe Rodeph Zedek in 1893 to form Kesher Israel. The former synagogue building is no longer standing. *Image courtesy of the Jacob Rader Marcus Center of the American Jewish Archives.*

Congregation Chevre Thillim Mishnayos, Auburn and Tulip Streets, Port Richmond section, Philadelphia, Pennsylvania. Former synagogue exterior view. Established in 1880, the synagogue was built sometime during the early twentieth century. This Orthodox congregation is no longer an active congregation. *Photograph courtesy of Arthur Rosenthol, 2007.*

Tifereth Israel of Parkside, 3940 West Girard Avenue, Philadelphia, Pennsylvania. Former synagogue exterior view. This Orthodox congregation in the Parkside section of West Philadelphia was formed in 1904. The congregation obtained the former building of the Parkside Republican Club and remodelled it for use as a synagogue in 1923, and again in 1934 after a fire. The congregation disbanded in the early 1960s. *Photograph by Julian H. Preisler, 1994.*

Tikvoh Chadoshoh Congregation, 5364 Chew Avenue, Philadelphia, Pennsylvania. Former synagogue exterior view. This Conservative congregation was established in 1942 and purchased the Teller Memorial building on the grounds of the former German Jewish Orphanage in 1951. By 1985, the congregation closed and most members joined the Oxford Circle Jewish Community Centre and Congregation Brith Israel. In 1989, these two congregations, which had merged previously, then merged with Adath Jeshurun in suburban Elkins Park. *Photograph by Julian H. Preisler, 1994.*

Unknown former synagogue, North Broad Street, Philadelphia, Pennsylvania. Exterior view. It is not known whether this building is still standing. *Photograph by Julian H. Preisler, 1994.*

Vilna Congregation, 509 Pine Street, Philadelphia, Pennsylvania. Current synagogue exterior view. This Orthodox congregation in the Society Hill section of Center City, Philadelphia, was established in 1904. The present building, a former residence, was purchased and remodeled for use as a synagogue circa 1916. The congregation is also known as Beis Haknesses Anshei Vilno. *Photograph by Julian H. Preisler, 2008.*

West Oak Lane Jewish Community Center, Thouron and Sedgewick Streets, Philadelphia, Pennsylvania. Former synagogue exterior view. This Conservative congregation in the West Oak Lane section of North Philadelphia was established in 1950. The synagogue was built in the late 1950s and is an excellent example of the Mid-Century Modern style. In 1978, the congregation closed and merged with Beth Sholom Congregation in suburban Elkins Park. *Photograph by Julian H. Preisler, 2008.*

West Oak Lane Jewish Community Center, Thouron and Sedgewick Streets, Philadelphia, Pennsylvania. Former synagogue exterior detail. *Photograph by Julian H. Preisler, 2008.*

West Philadelphia Jewish Community Center, Ludlow Street and West Cobbs Creek Parkway, Philadelphia, Pennsylvania. Former synagogue exterior view. This Conservative congregation in West Philadelphia was formed in 1923 through the merger of Beth Judah (founded 1905) and the West Philadelphia Hebrew School (founded 1914). The synagogue was built in 1927–28. In 1960, the synagogue closed, and many members joined Beth Hillel in suburban Wynnewood. *Photograph by Julian H. Preisler, 2008.*

West Philadelphia Jewish Community Center, Ludlow Street and West Cobbs Creek Parkway, Philadelphia, Pennsylvania. Former synagogue exterior front detail. *Photograph by Julian H. Preisler, 2008.*

B'nai Jacob Synagogue Center, Starr and Manavon Street, Phoenixville, Montgomery County, Pennsylvania. Current synagogue exterior view. This Conservative synagogue officially organized in 1912. The synagogue was built in 1957 and expanded in the late 1990s. *Photograph courtesy of Arthur Rosenthol, 2007.*

Congregation Mercy and Truth, 575 North Keim Street, Pottstown, Pennsylvania. Current synagogue exterior view. This Conservative congregation was formally established in 1892. The present synagogue was dedicated in 1962. *Photograph by Julian H. Preisler, 1993.*

Ohev Shalom of Bucks County, 944 Second Street Pike, Bucks County, Richboro, Pennsylvania. Current synagogue exterior view. This Conservative congregation was formed in 1976. The present synagogue was built in 1983 and expanded in the 1990s. The sanctuary is very environmentally friendly, with a large, passive solar collector on the roof that doubles as art with wonderful stained glass on the inside. *Photograph by Julian H. Preisler, 1993.*

Ohev Shalom of Bucks County, 944 Second Street Pike, Bucks County, Richboro, Pennsylvania. Current synagogue exterior detail. *Photograph by Julian H. Preisler, 1993.*

Congregation Beth Or, Penllyn Pike and Dager Road, Spring House, Montgomery County, Pennsylvania. Former synagogue exterior view. This Reform congregation was established in 1954 in Northwest Philadelphia. The former synagogue in Spring House was dedicated in 1974. In 2006, the congregation relocated to Maple Glen and built a large new synagogue. *Photograph by Julian H. Preisler, 1995.*

Congregation Ner Tamid–Delaware County Jewish Community Center, 300 Woodland Avenue, Springfield, Delaware County, Pennsylvania. Former synagogue exterior view. This Conservative congregation was established in 1957. The functional synagogue building was constructed in 1960. In 1992, the congregation closed and merged with Beth El Suburban in nearby Broomall, forming Congregation Beth El Ner Tamid. *Photograph by Julian H. Preisler, 1991.*

Temple Israel, Walnut Street and Bywood Avenue, Upper Darby, Delaware County, Pennsylvania. Former synagogue exterior front detail. This Conservative congregation was formed in 1945. The Colonial-style synagogue was built circa 1956. In 2000, Temple Israel closed and merged with Congregation Beth El Ner Tamid in suburban Broomal. *Photograph by Julian H. Preisler, 1992.*

Temple Israel, Walnut Street and Bywood Avenue, Upper Darby, Delaware County, Pennsylvania. Former synagogue exterior view. *Photograph by Julian H. Preisler, 1992.*

Congregation Ohev Shalom, 2 Chester Road, Wallingford, Delaware County, Pennsylvania. Current synagogue exterior view. This Conservative congregation was originally established in the city of Chester in 1891. The congregation relocated to suburban Wallingford and dedicated its new synagogue in 1965. The synagogue was designed by the noted American synagogue architect Percival Goodman, who had designed over fifty synagogues across the United States. *Photograph courtesy of Tom Stevick, 2007.*

Congregation Ohev Shalom, 2 Chester Road, Wallingford, Delaware County, Pennsylvania. Current synagogue sanctuary interior view, circa 1985. *Photograph from an Ohev Shalom membership booklet. Author's collection.*

Tiferes B'nai Israel Congregation, 2478 Street Road, Warrington, Bucks County, Pennsylvania. Current synagogue exterior view. This Reconstructionist congregation began around 1911 and was originally Orthodox. The congregation was chartered in 1924. The original synagogue was built in 1923 and is currently used as classrooms. An additon was built in the 1930s, and the current sanctuary was built in 1962. The building was recently listed as a "Warrington Historic Site" and a historical marker was placed at the synagogue. *Photograph by Julian H. Preisler, 2008.*

Kesher Israel Congregation, 206 North Church Street, West Chester, Chester County, Pennsylvania. Former synagogue exterior view. This Conservative congregation was established in the Borough of West Chester in 1914. Kesher Israel was originally formed as an Orthodox congregation. The former synagogue was built in 1924 and was one of the first synagogues designed by noted architect Norman N. Rice. In 1988, Kesher Israel built a new synagogue in the suburbs outside of the borough. *Photograph by Julian H. Preisler, 1994.*

Kesher Israel Congregation, 1000 Pottstown Pike, West Chester, Chester County, Pennsylvania. Current synagogue exterior side view. The synagogue was designed in the style reminiscent of the traditional wooden synagogues found in Eastern Europe. *Photograph by Julian H. Preisler, 1994.*

Kesher Israel Congregation, 1000 Pottstown Pike, West Chester, Chester County, Pennsylvania. Current synagogue exterior front view. *Photograph by Julian H. Preisler, 1994.*

Main Line Reform Temple–Beth Elohim, 410 Montgomery Avenue, Wynnewood, Montgomery County, Pennsylvania. Current synagogue exterior view. The first Reform congregation on the "Main Line," Beth Elohim was formed in 1952. The present Mid-Century Modern synagogue was dedicated in 1960. A large expansion and renovation project at the synagogue was completed in 2006. *Photograph by Julian H. Preisler, 1993.*

Main Line Reform Temple–Beth Elohim, 410 Montgomery Avenue, Wynnewood, Montgomery County, Pennsylvania. Current synagogue sanctuary interior view. *Photograph courtesy of Arthur Rosenthol, 2007.*

Congregation Beth Hamedrosh, 200 Haverford Road, Wynnewood, Montgomery County, Pennsylvania. Current synagogue exterior view. This Orthodox congregation was originally established in the Overbrook section of West Philadelphia in the 1950s. The present synagogue was built in 2007. The site was purchased in 2000 and included a 1922 stone house, which was part of the construction of the new synagogue complex. *Photograph courtesy of Arthur Rosenthol, 2007.*

Temple Beth Hillel Beth El, 1001 Remington Road, Wynnewood, Montgomery County, Pennsylvania. Current synagogue exterior view. This Conservative congregation was formed in suburban Wynnewood in 1958 as Beth Hillel. Most members of the West Philadelphia Jewish Center merged into Beth Hillel about 1960, when the former synagogue closed. Beth El of Philadelphia merged with Beth Hillel in 1970, forming the current congregation. The present synagogue was built in 1967 and was designed by noted architect Norman N. Rice. Major additions and renovations were done in 1990 and 2001. *Photograph courtesy of Arthur Rosenthol, 2007.*

Temple Beth Hillel–Beth El, 1001 Remington Road, Wynnewood, Montgomery County, Pennsylvania. Current synagogue exterior detail. *Photograph courtesy of Arthur Rosenthol, 2007.*

Congregation Beth El, 375 Stoney Hill Road, Yardley, Bucks County, Pennsylvania. Current synagogue exterior view. This Conservative congregation was established in 1953 in the Fallsington area of Bucks County, where the previous synagogue was located. The new building in Yardley was dedicated in 2008. *Photograph courtesy of Congregation Beth El and Karen Lewin, 2008.*

Yeadon Jewish Community Center–Congregation Beth Tefilah, West Cobbs Creek Parkway and Whitby Avenue, Yeadon, Delaware County, Pennsylvania. Former synagogue entrance view. This Conservative congregation was established about 1946. The former synagogue was built between the years 1946 and 1949, and was designed by Beryl Price. In 1991, the congregation closed and merged with the Suburban Jewish Community Center–B'nai Aaron Congregation in Havertown. *Photograph by Julian H. Preisler, 1990.*

# SOUTHERN NEW JERSEY SYNAGOGUES

Congregation Beth Abraham, 330 Fayette Street, Bridgeton, New Jersey. Former synagogue exterior. This Conservative/Reconstructionist congregation was established circa 1915. The synagogue building was constructed circa 1971. Congregation Beth Abraham recently closed and sold the building to the city, which will use it as court space and police offices. *Photograph by Julian H. Preisler, 1992.*

Congregation Beth El, Park Boulevard and Belleview, Camden, New Jersey. Former synagogue exterior view. This Conservative congregation was established in 1920. The former synagogue was built in 1924, but by the mid-1960s the congregation had relocated to suburban Cherry Hill. The former synagogue building in Camden was demolished circa 2000, and a Boys & Girls Club was built on the site. *Photograph by Julian H. Preisler, 1989.*

Congregation Beth Israel, 315 Grand Avenue, Camden, New Jersey. Former synagogue exterior. Established in 1929, this congregation's synagogue was built in 1956. In the 1970s, Beth Israel of Camden merged with Beth Jacob of Merchantville. The merged congregation worshiped in the Merchantville synagogue. A new synagogue was built in Cherry Hill in 1988, but the congregation soon disbanded in 1990. *Photograph by Julian H. Preisler, 1990.*

Congregation Beth Israel, 315 Grand Avenue, Camden, New Jersey. Former synagogue exterior detail. *Photograph by Julian H. Preisler, 1990.*

Sons of Israel Synagogue, Park Boulevard and Kaighn Avenue, Camden, New Jersey. Former synagogue exterior view. This Orthodox congregation was officially established in 1894 in Camden. The former synagogue was built in 1950. In 1971, the congregation relocated to suburban Cherry Hill, where it remains today. *Photograph by Julian H. Preisler, 1989.*

Sons of Israel Synagogue, Park Boulevard and Kaighn Avenue, Camden, New Jersey. Former synagogue additional exterior view. *Photograph by Julian H. Preisler, 1989.*

Sons of Israel Synagogue, Park Boulevard and Kaighn Avenue, Camden, New Jersey. Former synagogue front door detail. *Photograph by Julian H. Preisler, 1989.*

Congregation Beth El, 2901 West Chapel Avenue, Cherry Hill, New Jersey. Current synagogue exterior view. This modern synagogue was built in 1969, when the congregation relocated from Camden to suburban Cherry Hill. In 2009, Beth El plans to relocate to its newly constructed synagogue in nearby Voorhees. *Photograph by Julian H. Preisler, 1989.*

Congregation Beth El, 2901 West Chapel Avenue, Cherry Hill, New Jersey. Current synagogue additional exterior view. *Photograph by Julian H. Preisler, 1989.*

Temple Beth Sholom, 1901 Kresson Road, Cherry Hill, New Jersey. Current synagogue exterior view. This Conservative congregation was originally established in 1940 in nearby Haddon Heights. The current synagogue was built in 1989. *Photograph by Julian H. Preisler, 1989.*

Congregation M'Kor Shalom, 850 Evesham Road, Cherry Hill, New Jersey. Current synagogue exterior front view. This Reform congregation was established in 1974. M'Kor Shalom purchased the former synagogue of Beth Jacob–Beth Israel in 1990, when the former congregation disbanded. *Photograph by Julian H. Preisler, 1991.*

Congregation Sons of Israel, 720 Cooper Landing Road, Cherry Hill, New Jersey. Current synagogue exterior view. This new synagogue was dedicated in 1971, when the congregation relocated from Camden. *Photograph courtesy of Patricia Helfand, 2008.*

Temple Emanu-El, Cooper River Parkway and Donahue Street, Cherry Hill, New Jersey. Former synagogue exterior view. This Reform congregation was established in 1950. The synagogue was built in 1959, with a new temple built farther east in Cherry Hill in 1992. *Photograph by Julian H. Preisler, 1992.*

Temple Emanu-El, Springdale and Kresson Roads, Cherry Hill, New Jersey. Current synagogue exterior view. This large, new temple building was dedicated in 1992. *Photograph by Julian H. Preisler, 1992.*

Temple Beth Shalom, Green Street at White Horse Pike, Haddon Heights, New Jersey. Former synagogue exterior side view. Built in various stages between 1956 and 1962, the congregation is now located in Cherry Hill. *Photograph by Julian H. Preisler, 1989.*

Congregation Beth Jacob–Beth Israel, 109 East Maple Avenue, Merchantville, New Jersey. Former synagogue exterior side view. Beth Jacob was established as the Hebrew Congregation of Merchantville sometime prior to 1942. This former synagogue building was constructed in the 1950s or 1960s. Beth Jacob of Merchantville and Beth Israel of Camden merged in the 1970s and worshiped in the Merchantville building. In 1988, they built a new synagogue in nearby Cherry Hill. The congregation disbanded in 1990, and the Cherry Hill building was purchased by M'Kor Shalom. It is believed that the Merchantville building was torn down prior to 2008 and replaced with new homes. *Photograph by Julian H. Preisler, 1990.*

Congregation Beth Jacob–Beth Israel, 109 East Maple Avenue, Merchantville, New Jersey. Former synagogue exterior front view. *Photograph by Julian H. Preisler, 1990.*

Congregation Beth Hillel, Third and Oak Street, Millville, New Jersey. Former synagogue exterior view. This Conservative synagogue was established about 1929 and closed between 1992 and 2008. The former synagogue building is now a church. *Photograph by Julian H. Preisler, 1992.*

Temple Har Zion, High and Ridgeway Streets, Mount Holly, New Jersey. Current synagogue exterior view. Established about 1937, this Mid-Century Modern synagogue was built in the early 1960s. Har Zion follows a Conservative/Renewal worship style. *Photograph by Julian H. Preisler, 1992.*

Shaari Zedek Congregation, 99 North Broad Street, Penns Grove, New Jersey. Former synagogue exterior view. Located across the Delaware River from Wilmington, the congregation was established in 1910 as an Orthodox congregation. The synagogue was built in 1901 as a Catholic church and was purchased by Shaari Zedek in 1923. Shaari Zedek Congregation is thought to have disbanded sometime in the 1990s. *Photograph by Julian H. Preisler, 1990.*

Agudath Achim, 2196 South Main Road Vineland, New Jersey. Former synagogue exterior view. It is not known whether this Orthodox synagogue has disbanded or is currently functioning on a limited basis. *Photograph courtesy of Bill McLean, 2007.*

Congregation Beth Israel, 1015 East Park Avenue, Vineland, New Jersey. Current synagogue exterior view. This Conservative congregation was established in 1923. The modern synagogue was dedicated in 1958 and is the largest in Vineland. *Photograph courtesy of Bill McLean, 2007.*

Sons of Jacob Synagogue, 321 West Grape Street, Vineland, New Jersey. Current synagogue exterior view. Sons of Jacob is the oldest Jewish congregation in Vineland. Its synagogue, which is Orthodox in worship style, was built in 1908. *Photograph courtesy of Bill McLean, 2007.*

Temple Emanu-El, John F. Kennedy Way, Willingboro, New Jersey. Former synagogue exterior view. Temple Emanu-El is thought to have begun in the 1960s in Willingboro (Levittown). Because of demographic shifts, the congregation built a new synagogue in nearby Mount Laurel in 1997 and became Adath Emanu-El. The other synagogue that existed in Willingboro, Beth Torah, closed after 1991. *Photograph by Julian H. Preisler, 1991.*

Woodbine Brotherhood Synagogue, 610 Washington Avenue, Woodbine, New Jersey. Former synagogue exterior view. This congregation was established in 1893 by newly arrived Jewish factory workers and Jewish farmers. The ornate Orthodox synagogue was dedicated in 1896. In 2003, the former synagogue building, which no longer housed a functioning Jewish congregation, became the Sam Azeez Museum of Woodbine Heritage. *Photograph by Julian H. Preisler, 1994.*

Beth Israel Congregation, 246 King Street, Woodbury, New Jersey. Current synagogue exterior view. Established in 1928, the synagogue was initially built during the 1950s, a chapel was added in 1972 and the synagogue was renovated and expanded in the 1980s. Beth Israel is an unaffiliated Progressive congregation. *Photograph by Julian H. Preisler, 1992.*

# DELAWARE SYNAGOGUES

Beth Sholom Congregation, Queen and Clara Streets, Dover, Delaware. Current synagogue exterior view. Established as a Conservative congregation in 1947, the present synagogue was built in 1963. It is the only synagogue in Kent County. *Photograph by Julian H. Preisler, 1995.*

Temple Beth El, Amstel Avenue, Newark, Delaware. Former synagogue exterior view. Established in 1954, the congregation built this Mid-Century Modern synagogue in 1963. The present synagogue of this Reconstructionist congregation was built in 1984. *Photograph by Julian H. Preisler, 1995.*

Adas Kodesch Congregation, Sixth and French Streets, Wilmington, Delaware. Former synagogue exterior view, 1941. Established in 1885, this synagogue was dedicated in 1908. The congregation merged with the Chesed Shel Emeth Congregation in 1957 and dedicated a new modern synagogue on Washington Street Extension in 1963. The French Street building is no longer standing. The current congregation is an independent Traditional synagogue. *Photograph courtesy of the Jewish Historical Society of Delaware.*

Adas Kodesch Congregation, Sixth and French Streets, Wilmington, Delaware. Former synagogue interior view, 1941. *Photograph courtesy of the Jewish Historical Society of Delaware.*

Adas Kodesch Shel Emeth Congregation, Washington Street Extension and Torah Way. Current synagogue exterior view. Designed by the noted Jewish synagogue architect Percival Goodman, this synagogue was dedicated in 1963. *Photograph courtesy of Debra Steinberg, 2008.*

Congregation Beth Emeth, 300 West Lea Boulevard, Wilmington, Delaware. Current synagogue exterior side view. This Reform congregation was established in 1906. Beth Emeth completed this building in 1954. An extensive expansion and remodeling was completed in 2008. *Photograph courtesy of Debra Steinberg, 2008.*

Congregation Beth Emeth, 300 West Lea Boulevard, Wilmington, Delaware. Current synagogue exterior front view detail. *Photograph by Julian H. Preisler, 1990.*

Congregation Beth Emeth, 300 West Lea Boulevard, Wilmington, Delaware. Current sanctuary interior view, 2008. *Photograph courtesy of Debra Steinberg, 2008.*

Congregation Beth Emeth, 904 Washington Street, Wilmington, Delaware. Former synagogue drawing, undated. Built in 1908, this building is no longer standing. It was known as the "Temple of Truth." *Photograph courtesy of the Jewish Historical Society of Delaware.*

Congregation Beth Shalom, Eighteenth Street and Baynard Boulevard, Wilmington, Delaware. Current synagogue exterior view. This Conservative congregation was established in 1922. The current synagogue was built in 1954 and was expanded and renovated in 2008. *Photograph courtesy of Debra Steinberg, 2008.*

Congregation Beth Shalom, Eighteenth Street and Baynard Boulevard, Wilmington, Delaware. Sanctuary interior view. *Photograph courtesy of Debra Steinberg, 2008.*

Congregation Beth Shalom, Eighteenth Street and Baynard Boulevard, Wilmington, Delaware. Sanctuary interior view, 1950s. *Photograph courtesy of the Jewish Historical Society of Delaware.*

Congregation Beth Shalom, Eighteenth Street and Baynard Boulevard, Wilmington, Delaware. Former synagogue exterior view, 1930s. This remodeled building was used as the synagogue until the current synagogue was dedicated in 1954. The building, which stood across the street from the current synagogue, is no longer standing. *Photograph courtesy of the Jewish Historical Society of Delaware.*

Congregation Beth Shalom, Eighteenth Street and Baynard Boulevard, Wilmington, Delaware. Architect's drawing of proposed synagogue, 1949. *Courtesy of the Jewish Historical Society of Delaware.*

Chesed Shel Emeth Congregation, Third and Shipley Streets, Wilmington, Delaware. Former synagogue exterior view, circa 1930s. Established in 1901, the synagogue was dedicated in 1915. The congregation merged with Adas Kodesch in 1957, and together they built the new facility on Washington Street Extension in 1963. The Shipley Street building is no longer standing. *Photograph courtesy of the Jewish Historical Society of Delaware.*

Chesed Shel Emeth Congregation, Third and Shipley Streets, Wilmington, Delaware. Drawing of proposed new synagogue, 1950s. This building was never built due to the merger of Chesed Shel Emeth and Adas Kodesch in 1957. *Courtesy of the Jewish Historical Society of Delaware.*

# About the Author

Mr. Preisler is a researcher, genealogist and author residing in the Eastern Panhandle of West Virginia. A graduate of the University of Florida and Mary Washington College, he has a broad background in archives and history, and has been a professional genealogist and researcher for over eighteen years. The son of Holocaust survivors from Germany and the Czech Republic, Julian is a native of Detroit, Michigan, and has had an interest in Jewish history/genealogy and synagogue architecture for over twenty-five years. He has published several books and has written articles for a variety of Jewish and non-Jewish newspapers. Mr. Preisler has also been involved in photographing and indexing U.S. Jewish cemeteries for many years.